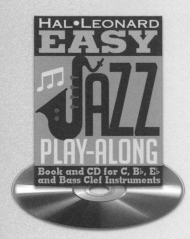

Hal·Leonard

EASY JAZZ PLAY-ALONG

Book and CD for C, B♭, E♭ and Bass Clef Instruments

Volume 6

CHRISTMAS STANDARDS

T0078799

Hal•Leonard
EASY
JAZZ
PLAY-ALONG

Book and CD for C, B♭, E♭
and Bass Clef Instruments

CHRISTMAS STANDARDS

18 Classics
for Beginning Jazz Musicians

Recorded by Ric Probst at Tanner Monagle Studio
Piano: Mark Davis
Bass: Jeff Hamann
Drums: Dave Bayles

ISBN 978-1-4768-0869-7

7777 W. BLUEMOUND RD. P.O. BOX 13819 MILWAUKEE, WI 53213

Visit Hal Leonard Online at
www.halleonard.com

CONTENTS

TITLE	PAGE NUMBERS			
	C Treble Instruments	B♭ Instruments	E♭ Instruments	C Bass Instruments
All I Want for Christmas Is My Two Front Teeth	6	32	58	84
Blue Christmas	8	34	60	86
Christmas Time Is Here	7	33	59	85
Do You Hear What I Hear	10	36	62	88
Feliz Navidad	12	38	64	90
Happy Holiday	11	37	63	89
Have Yourself a Merry Little Christmas	14	40	66	92
Here Comes Santa Claus (Right Down Santa Claus Lane)	15	41	67	93
A Holly Jolly Christmas	16	42	68	94
I Saw Mommy Kissing Santa Claus	18	44	70	96
I'll Be Home for Christmas	19	45	71	97
Jingle Bell Rock	20	46	72	98
Let It Snow! Let It Snow! Let It Snow!	22	48	74	100
Rudolph the Red-Nosed Reindeer	24	50	76	102
Santa Claus Is Comin' to Town	26	52	78	104
Silver and Gold	28	54	80	106
Silver Bells	29	55	81	107
Winter Wonderland	30	56	82	108

BOOK

CONTENTS

TITLE	CD Track Number
All I Want for Christmas Is My Two Front Teeth	1
Blue Christmas	2
Christmas Time Is Here	3
Do You Hear What I Hear	4
Feliz Navidad	5
Happy Holiday	6
Have Yourself a Merry Little Christmas	7
Here Comes Santa Claus (Right Down Santa Claus Lane)	8
A Holly Jolly Christmas	9
I Saw Mommy Kissing Santa Claus	10
I'll Be Home for Christmas	11
Jingle Bell Rock	12
Let It Snow! Let It Snow! Let It Snow!	13
Rudolph the Red-Nosed Reindeer	14
Santa Claus Is Comin' to Town	15
Silver and Gold	16
Silver Bells	17
Winter Wonderland	18
B♭ Tuning Notes	19

CD

ALL I WANT FOR CHRISTMAS IS MY TWO FRONT TEETH

C VERSION

WORDS AND MUSIC BY
DON GARDNER

Christmas Time Is Here
FROM A CHARLIE BROWN CHRISTMAS

C VERSION

Words by Lee Mendelson
Music by Vince Guaraldi

Blue Christmas

C Version

Words and Music by Billy Hayes and Jay Johnson

Do You Hear What I Hear

C Version

Words and Music by Noel Regney
and Gloria Shayne

HAPPY HOLIDAY
FROM THE MOTION PICTURE IRVING BERLIN'S HOLIDAY INN

C VERSION

Words and Music by
Irving Berlin

Feliz Navidad

C Version

Music and Lyrics by
JOSÉ FELICIANO

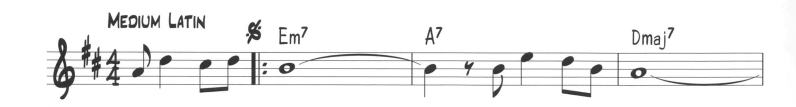

Have Yourself a Merry Little Christmas

FROM MEET ME IN ST. LOUIS

C VERSION

Words and Music by Hugh Martin and Ralph Blane

Here Comes Santa Claus
(Right Down Santa Claus Lane)

C Version

Words and Music by Gene Autry
and Oakley Haldeman

A HOLLY JOLLY CHRISTMAS

C VERSION

Music and Lyrics by
Johnny Marks

Medium Dixie Swing

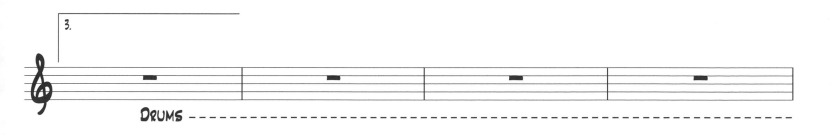

I Saw Mommy Kissing Santa Claus

C Version

Words and Music by
Tommie Connor

I'LL BE HOME FOR CHRISTMAS

C VERSION

WORDS AND MUSIC BY KIM GANNON
AND WALTER KENT

Jingle Bell Rock

C Version

Words and Music by Joe Beal
and Jim Boothe

Let It Snow! Let It Snow! Let It Snow!

C Version

Words by Sammy Cahn
Music by Jule Styne

Rudolph the Red-Nosed Reindeer

C Version

Music and Lyrics by
Johnny Marks

25

Santa Claus Is Comin' To Town

C Version

Words by Haven Gillespie
Music by J. Fred Coots

SILVER AND GOLD

C VERSION

MUSIC AND LYRICS BY
JOHNNY MARKS

Silver Bells

FROM THE PARAMOUNT PICTURE THE LEMON DROP KID

C Version

WORDS AND MUSIC BY JAY LIVINGSTON
AND RAY EVANS

Winter Wonderland

C Version

Words by Dick Smith
Music by Felix Bernard

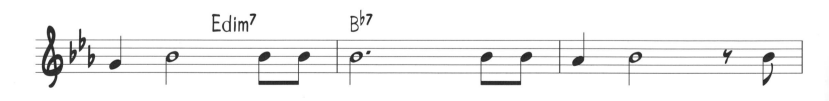

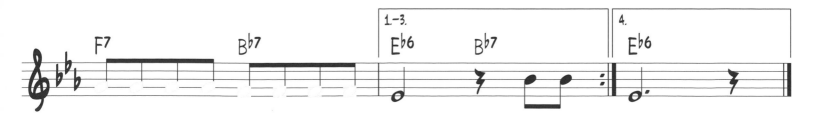

ALL I WANT FOR CHRISTMAS IS MY TWO FRONT TEETH

Bb Version

Words and Music by
Don Gardner

Christmas Time Is Here
FROM A CHARLIE BROWN CHRISTMAS

Bb VERSION

WORDS BY LEE MENDELSON
MUSIC BY VINCE GUARALDI

Blue Christmas

Bb Version

Words and Music by Billy Hayes
and Jay Johnson

Do You Hear What I Hear

Bb Version

Words and Music by Noel Regney
and Gloria Shayne

HAPPY HOLIDAY

FROM THE MOTION PICTURE IRVING BERLIN'S HOLIDAY INN

Bb VERSION

WORDS AND MUSIC BY
IRVING BERLIN

Feliz Navidad

Bb Version

Music and Lyrics by
José Feliciano

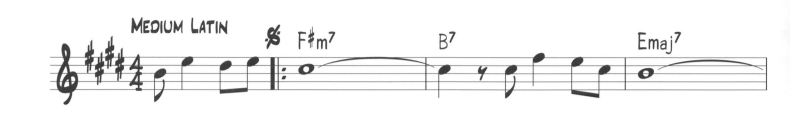

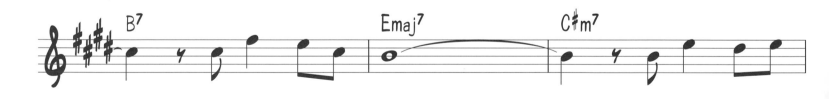

Have Yourself a Merry Little Christmas

FROM MEET ME IN ST. LOUIS

B♭ VERSION

WORDS AND MUSIC BY HUGH MARTIN
AND RALPH BLANE

HERE COMES SANTA CLAUS
(Right Down Santa Claus Lane)

Bb Version

Words and Music by Gene Autry
and Oakley Haldeman

A Holly Jolly Christmas

B♭ Version

Music and Lyrics by
Johnny Marks

I Saw Mommy Kissing Santa Claus

Bb Version

Words and Music by
Tommie Connor

I'll Be Home For Christmas

Bb Version

Words and Music by Kim Gannon
and Walter Kent

JINGLE BELL ROCK

Bb VERSION

WORDS AND MUSIC BY JOE BEAL
AND JIM BOOTHE

MEDIUM SHUFFLE

LET IT SNOW! LET IT SNOW! LET IT SNOW!

B♭ Version

Words by Sammy Cahn
Music by Jule Styne

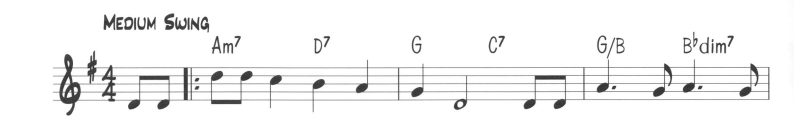

Rudolph the Red-Nosed Reindeer

Bb Version

Music and Lyrics by
Johnny Marks

Santa Claus Is Comin' to Town

Bb Version

Words by Haven Gillespie
Music by J. Fred Coots

SILVER AND GOLD

B♭ VERSION

MUSIC AND LYRICS BY
JOHNNY MARKS

Silver Bells
FROM THE PARAMOUNT PICTURE THE LEMON DROP KID

Bb VERSION

WORDS AND MUSIC BY JAY LIVINGSTON
AND RAY EVANS

Winter Wonderland

B♭ Version

Words by Dick Smith
Music by Felix Bernard

Medium Swing

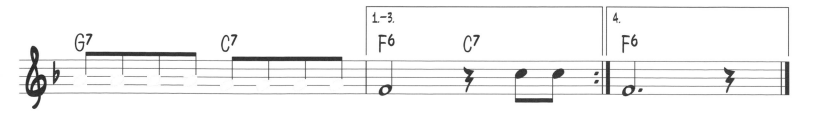

ALL I WANT FOR CHRISTMAS IS MY TWO FRONT TEETH

E♭ Version

Words and Music by
Don Gardner

Christmas Time Is Here
FROM A CHARLIE BROWN CHRISTMAS

Eb Version

Words by Lee Mendelson
Music by Vince Guaraldi

Blue Christmas

E♭ Version

Words and Music by Billy Hayes
and Jay Johnson

Do You Hear What I Hear

Eb Version

Words and Music by Noel Regney
and Gloria Shayne

HAPPY HOLIDAY

FROM THE MOTION PICTURE IRVING BERLIN'S HOLIDAY INN

Eb VERSION

WORDS AND MUSIC BY
IRVING BERLIN

Feliz Navidad

E♭ Version

Music and Lyrics by
José Feliciano

Medium Latin

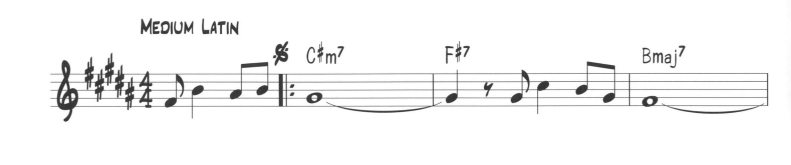

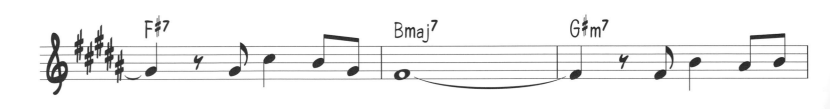

Have Yourself a Merry Little Christmas

FROM MEET ME IN ST. LOUIS

E♭ Version

Words and Music by Hugh Martin
and Ralph Blane

Here Comes Santa Claus
(Right Down Santa Claus Lane)

Eb Version

Words and Music by Gene Autry
and Oakley Haldeman

Medium Swing

A Holly Jolly Christmas

Eb Version

Music and Lyrics by
Johnny Marks

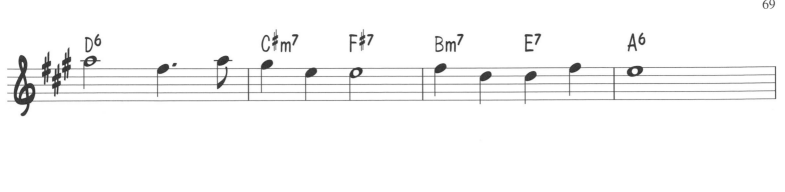

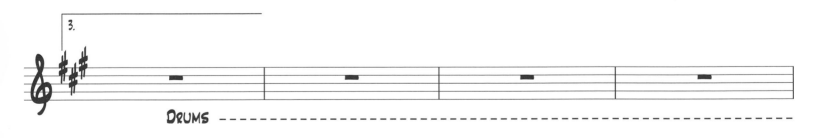

I Saw Mommy Kissing Santa Claus

Eb Version

Words and Music by
Tommie Connor

I'll Be Home for Christmas

E♭ Version

Words and Music by Kim Gannon
and Walter Kent

Jingle Bell Rock

Eb Version

Words and Music by Joe Beal
and Jim Boothe

Let It Snow! Let It Snow! Let It Snow!

Eb Version

Words by Sammy Cahn
Music by Jule Styne

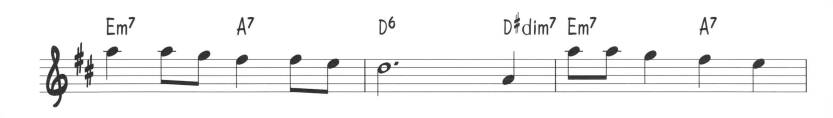

Rudolph the Red-Nosed Reindeer

Eb Version

Music and Lyrics by
Johnny Marks

Santa Claus Is Comin' to Town

Eb Version

Words by Haven Gillespie
Music by J. Fred Coots

SILVER AND GOLD

E♭ Version

Music and Lyrics by
Johnny Marks

Silver Bells
from the Paramount Picture The Lemon Drop Kid

Eb Version

Words and Music by Jay Livingston
and Ray Evans

Winter Wonderland

Eb Version

Words by Dick Smith
Music by Felix Bernard

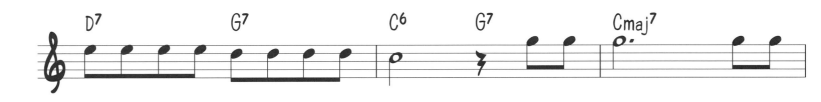

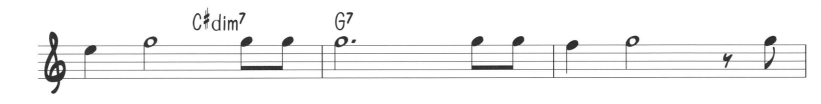

ALL I WANT FOR CHRISTMAS IS MY TWO FRONT TEETH

℈: VERSION

Words and Music by
Don Gardner

Christmas Time Is Here
FROM A CHARLIE BROWN CHRISTMAS

Words by Lee Mendelson
Music by Vince Guaraldi

Blue Christmas

Version

Words and Music by Billy Hayes
and Jay Johnson

INTRODUCTION
SOFT LATIN

Do You Hear What I Hear

C: Version

Words and Music by Noel Regney
and Gloria Shayne

HAPPY HOLIDAY

FROM THE MOTION PICTURE IRVING BERLIN'S HOLIDAY INN

♭ Version

WORDS AND MUSIC BY
IRVING BERLIN

Feliz Navidad

𝄢 Version

Music and Lyrics by
José Feliciano

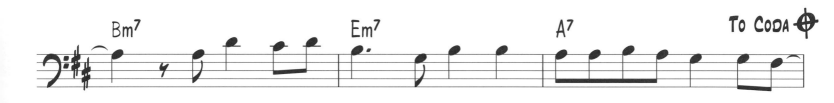

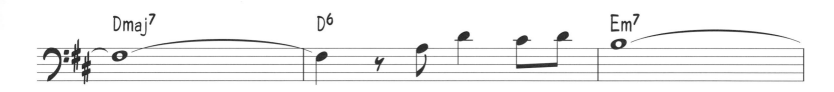

Have Yourself a Merry Little Christmas

FROM MEET ME IN ST. LOUIS

℃ Version

Words and Music by Hugh Martin
and Ralph Blane

HERE COMES SANTA CLAUS
(Right Down Santa Claus Lane)

Words and Music by Gene Autry
and Oakley Haldeman

A Holly Jolly Christmas

Music and Lyrics by
Johnny Marks

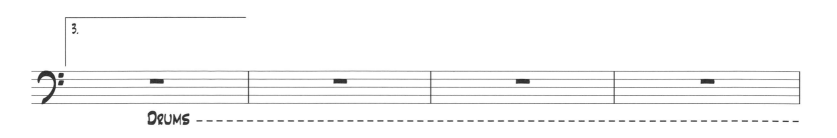

I Saw Mommy Kissing Santa Claus

𝄢 Version

Words and Music by
TOMMIE CONNOR

I'll Be Home For Christmas

C Version

Words and Music by Kim Gannon
and Walter Kent

Jingle Bell Rock

♭: Version

WORDS AND MUSIC BY JOE BEAL
AND JIM BOOTHE

Let It Snow! Let It Snow! Let It Snow!

𝄢 Version

Words by Sammy Cahn
Music by Jule Styne

Rudolph the Red-Nosed Reindeer

 Version

Music and Lyrics by
Johnny Marks

Santa Claus Is Comin' To Town

℣ Version

Words by Haven Gillespie
Music by J. Fred Coots

Silver and Gold

𝄢 Version

Music and Lyrics by
Johnny Marks

Silver Bells

FROM THE PARAMOUNT PICTURE THE LEMON DROP KID

𝄢 Version

WORDS AND MUSIC BY JAY LIVINGSTON
AND RAY EVANS

Winter Wonderland

℧: Version

Words by Dick Smith
Music by Felix Bernard

Presenting the Hal Leonard JAZZ PLAY-ALONG SERIES

For use with all B-flat, E-flat, Bass Clef and C instruments, the Jazz Play-Along® Series is the ultimate learning tool for all jazz musicians. With musician-friendly lead sheets, melody cues, and other split-track choices on the included CD, these first-of-a-kind packages help you master improvisation while playing some of the greatest tunes of all time. FOR STUDY, each tune includes a split track with: melody cue with proper style and inflection • professional rhythm tracks • choruses for soloing • removable bass part • removable piano part. FOR PERFORMANCE, each tune also has: an additional full stereo accompaniment track (no melody) • additional choruses for soloing.

1A. MAIDEN VOYAGE/ALL BLUES
00843158 ....$15.99

1. DUKE ELLINGTON
00841644.............................$16.95

2. MILES DAVIS
00841645.............................$16.95

3. THE BLUES
00841646.............................$16.99

4. JAZZ BALLADS
00841691.............................$16.99

5. BEST OF BEBOP
00841689.............................$16.95

6. JAZZ CLASSICS WITH EASY CHANGES
00841690.............................$16.99

7. ESSENTIAL JAZZ STANDARDS
00843000.............................$16.99

8. ANTONIO CARLOS JOBIM AND THE ART OF THE BOSSA NOVA
00843001.............................$16.95

9. DIZZY GILLESPIE
00843002.............................$16.99

10. DISNEY CLASSICS
00843003.............................$16.99

11. RODGERS AND HART FAVORITES
00843004.............................$16.99

12. ESSENTIAL JAZZ CLASSICS
00843005.............................$16.99

13. JOHN COLTRANE
00843006.............................$16.95

14. IRVING BERLIN
00843007.............................$15.99

15. RODGERS & HAMMERSTEIN
00843008.............................$15.99

16. COLE PORTER
00843009.............................$15.95

17. COUNT BASIE
00843010.............................$16.95

18. HAROLD ARLEN
00843011.............................$15.95

19. COOL JAZZ
00843012.............................$15.95

20. CHRISTMAS CAROLS
00843080.............................$14.95

21. RODGERS AND HART CLASSICS
00843014.............................$14.95

22. WAYNE SHORTER
00843015.............................$16.95

23. LATIN JAZZ
00843016.............................$16.95

24. EARLY JAZZ STANDARDS
00843017.............................$14.95

25. CHRISTMAS JAZZ
00843018.............................$16.95

26. CHARLIE PARKER
00843019.............................$16.95

27. GREAT JAZZ STANDARDS
00843020.............................$16.99

28. BIG BAND ERA
00843021.............................$15.99

29. LENNON AND MCCARTNEY
00843022.............................$16.95

30. BLUES' BEST
00843023.............................$15.99

31. JAZZ IN THREE
00843024.............................$15.99

32. BEST OF SWING
00843025.............................$15.99

33. SONNY ROLLINS
00843029.............................$15.95

34. ALL TIME STANDARDS
00843030.............................$15.99

35. BLUESY JAZZ
00843031.............................$16.99

36. HORACE SILVER
00843032.............................$16.99

37. BILL EVANS
00843033.............................$16.95

38. YULETIDE JAZZ
00843034.............................$16.95

39. "ALL THE THINGS YOU ARE" & MORE JEROME KERN SONGS
00843035.............................$15.99

40. BOSSA NOVA
00843036.............................$16.99

41. CLASSIC DUKE ELLINGTON
00843037.............................$16.99

42. GERRY MULLIGAN FAVORITES
00843038.............................$16.99

43. GERRY MULLIGAN CLASSICS
00843039.............................$16.99

44. OLIVER NELSON
00843040.............................$16.95

45. JAZZ AT THE MOVIES
00843041.............................$15.99

46. BROADWAY JAZZ STANDARDS
00843042.............................$15.99

47. CLASSIC JAZZ BALLADS
00843043.............................$15.99

48. BEBOP CLASSICS
00843044.............................$16.99

49. MILES DAVIS STANDARDS
00843045.............................$16.95

50. GREAT JAZZ CLASSICS
00843046.............................$15.99

51. UP-TEMPO JAZZ
00843047.............................$15.99

52. STEVIE WONDER
00843048.............................$16.99

53. RHYTHM CHANGES
00843049.............................$15.99

54. "MOONLIGHT IN VERMONT" AND OTHER GREAT STANDARDS
00843050.............................$15.99

55. BENNY GOLSON
00843052.............................$15.95

56. "GEORGIA ON MY MIND" & OTHER SONGS BY HOAGY CARMICHAEL
00843056.............................$15.99

57. VINCE GUARALDI
00843057.............................$16.99

58. MORE LENNON AND MCCARTNEY
00843059.............................$16.99

59. SOUL JAZZ
00843060.............................$16.99

60. DEXTER GORDON
00843061.............................$15.95

61. MONGO SANTAMARIA
00843062.............................$15.95

62. JAZZ-ROCK FUSION
00843063.............................$16.99

63. CLASSICAL JAZZ
00843064 .... $14.95

64. TV TUNES
00843065 .... $14.95

65. SMOOTH JAZZ
00843066 .... $16.99

66. A CHARLIE BROWN CHRISTMAS
00843067 .... $16.99

67. CHICK COREA
00843068 .... $15.95

68. CHARLES MINGUS
00843069 .... $16.95

69. CLASSIC JAZZ
00843071 .... $15.99

70. THE DOORS
00843072 .... $14.95

71. COLE PORTER CLASSICS
00843073 .... $14.95

72. CLASSIC JAZZ BALLADS
00843074 .... $15.99

73. JAZZ/BLUES
00843075 .... $14.95

74. BEST JAZZ CLASSICS
00843076 .... $15.99

75. PAUL DESMOND
00843077 .... $15.99

76. BROADWAY JAZZ BALLADS
00843078 .... $15.99

77. JAZZ ON BROADWAY
00843079 .... $15.99

78. STEELY DAN
00843070 .... $15.99

79. MILES DAVIS CLASSICS
00843081 .... $15.99

80. JIMI HENDRIX
00843083 .... $16.99

81. FRANK SINATRA – CLASSICS
00843084 .... $15.99

82. FRANK SINATRA – STANDARDS
00843085 .... $15.99

83. ANDREW LLOYD WEBBER
00843104 .... $14.95

84. BOSSA NOVA CLASSICS
00843105 .... $14.95

85. MOTOWN HITS
00843109 .... $14.95

86. BENNY GOODMAN
00843110 .... $15.99

87. DIXIELAND
00843111 .... $14.95

88. DUKE ELLINGTON FAVORITES
00843112 .... $14.95

89. IRVING BERLIN FAVORITES
00843113 .... $14.95

90. THELONIOUS MONK CLASSICS
00841262 .... $16.99

91. THELONIOUS MONK FAVORITES
00841263 .... $16.99

92. LEONARD BERNSTEIN
00450134 .... $15.99

93. DISNEY FAVORITES
00843142 .... $14.99

94. RAY
00843143 .... $14.99

95. JAZZ AT THE LOUNGE
00843144 .... $14.99

96. LATIN JAZZ STANDARDS
00843145 .... $15.99

97. MAYBE I'M AMAZED*
00843148 .... $15.99

98. DAVE FRISHBERG
00843149 .... $15.99

99. SWINGING STANDARDS
00843150 .... $14.99

100. LOUIS ARMSTRONG
00740423 .... $16.99

101. BUD POWELL
00843152 .... $14.99

102. JAZZ POP
00843153 .... $14.99

103. ON GREEN DOLPHIN STREET & OTHER JAZZ CLASSICS
00843154 .... $14.99

104. ELTON JOHN
00843155 .... $14.99

105. SOULFUL JAZZ
00843151 .... $15.99

106. SLO' JAZZ
00843117 .... $14.99

107. MOTOWN CLASSICS
00843116 .... $14.99

108. JAZZ WALTZ
00843159 .... $15.99

109. OSCAR PETERSON
00843160 .... $16.99

110. JUST STANDARDS
00843161 .... $15.99

111. COOL CHRISTMAS
00843162 .... $15.99

112. PAQUITO D'RIVERA – LATIN JAZZ*
48020662 .... $16.99

113. PAQUITO D'RIVERA – BRAZILIAN JAZZ*
48020663 .... $19.99

114. MODERN JAZZ QUARTET FAVORITES
00843163 .... $15.99

115. THE SOUND OF MUSIC
00843164 .... $15.99

116. JACO PASTORIUS
00843165 .... $15.99

117. ANTONIO CARLOS JOBIM – MORE HITS
00843166 .... $15.99

118. BIG JAZZ STANDARDS COLLECTION
00843167 .... $27.50

119. JELLY ROLL MORTON
00843168 .... $15.99

120. J.S. BACH
00843169 .... $15.99

121. DJANGO REINHARDT
00843170 .... $15.99

122. PAUL SIMON
00843182 .... $16.99

123. BACHARACH & DAVID
00843185 .... $15.99

124. JAZZ-ROCK HORN HITS
00843186 .... $15.99

126. COUNT BASIE CLASSICS
00843157 .... $15.99

127. CHUCK MANGIONE
00843188 .... $15.99

128. VOCAL STANDARDS (LOW VOICE)
00843189 .... $15.99

129. VOCAL STANDARDS (HIGH VOICE)
00843190 .... $15.99

130. VOCAL JAZZ (LOW VOICE)
00843191 .... $15.99

131. VOCAL JAZZ (HIGH VOICE)
00843192 .... $15.99

132. STAN GETZ ESSENTIALS
00843193 .... $15.99

133. STAN GETZ FAVORITES
00843194 .... $15.99

134. NURSERY RHYMES*
00843196 .... $17.99

135. JEFF BECK
00843197 .... $15.99

136. NAT ADDERLEY
00843198 .... $15.99

137. WES MONTGOMERY
00843199 .... $15.99

138. FREDDIE HUBBARD
00843200 .... $15.99

139. JULIAN "CANNONBALL" ADDERLEY
00843201 .... $15.99

140. JOE ZAWINUL
00843202 .... $15.99

141. BILL EVANS STANDARDS
00843156 .... $15.99

142. CHARLIE PARKER GEMS
00843222 .... $15.99

150. JAZZ IMPROV BASICS
00843195 .... $19.99

151. MODERN JAZZ QUARTET CLASSICS
00843209 .... $15.99

152. J.J. JOHNSON
00843210 .... $15.99

154. HENRY MANCINI
00843213 .... $14.99

155. SMOOTH JAZZ CLASSICS
00843215 .... $15.99

156. THELONIOUS MONK – EARLY GEMS
00843216 .... $15.99

157. HYMNS
00843217 .... $15.99

158. JAZZ COVERS ROCK
00843219 .... $15.99

159. MOZART
00843220 .... $15.99

162. BIG CHRISTMAS COLLECTION
00843221 .... $24.99

*These CDs do not include split tracks.

0312

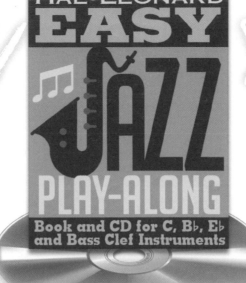

HAL•LEONARD EASY Jazz PLAY-ALONG

Book and CD for C, B♭, E♭ and Bass Clef Instruments

IMPROVISING IS EASIER THAN EVER

with this new series for beginning jazz musicians. The Hal Leonard Easy Jazz Play-Along Series includes songs with accessible chord changes and features recordings with novice-friendly tempos. Just follow the streamlined lead sheets in the book and play along with the professionally recorded backing tracks on the CD. The audio CD is playable on any CD player. For PC and Mac computer users, the CD is enhanced so you can adjust the recording to any tempo without changing pitch!

1. FIRST JAZZ SONGS
Book/CD Pack

All of Me • All the Things You Are • Autumn Leaves • C-Jam Blues • Comin' Home Baby • Footprints • The Girl from Ipanema (Garôta De Ipanema) • Killer Joe • Little Sunflower • Milestones • Mr. P.C. • On Green Dolphin Street • One for Daddy-O • Reunion Blues • Satin Doll • There Will Never Be Another You • Tune Up • Watermelon Man.

00843225 B♭, E♭, C & Bass Clef Instruments $19.99

2. STANDARDS FOR STARTERS
Book/CD Pack

Don't Get Around Much Anymore • Exactly like You • Fly Me to the Moon (In Other Words) • Have You Met Miss Jones? • Honeysuckle Rose • I Remember You • If I Should Lose You • It Could Happen to You • Moon River • My Favorite Things • On a Slow Boat to China • Out of Nowhere • Softly As in a Morning Sunrise • Speak Low • The Very Thought of You • Watch What Happens • The Way You Look Tonight • Yesterdays.

00843226 B♭, E♭, C & Bass Clef Instruments $19.99

3. EASY JAZZ CLASSICS
Book/CD Pack

Afternoon in Paris • Doxy • 500 Miles High • Girl Talk • Holy Land • Impressions • In Walked Bud • The Jive Samba • Lady Bird • Maiden Voyage • Mercy, Mercy, Mercy • My Little Suede Shoes • Recorda-Me • St. Thomas • Solar • Song for My Father • Stolen Moments • Sunny.

00843227 B♭, E♭, C & Bass Clef Instruments $19.99

4. BASIC BLUES
Book/CD Pack

All Blues • Birk's Works • Bloomdido • Blue Seven • Blue Train (Blue Trane) • Blues in the Closet • Cousin Mary • Freddie Freeloader • The Jody Grind • Jumpin' with Symphony Sid • Nostalgia in Times Square • Now See How You Are • Now's the Time • Sonnymoon for Two • Tenor Madness • Things Ain't What They Used to Be • Turnaround • Two Degrees East, Three Degrees West.

00843228 B♭, E♭, C & Bass Clef Instruments $19.99

5. EASY LATIN CLASSICS
Book/CD Pack

Baia (Bahía) • Begin the Beguine • Black Orpheus • Flamingo • Gentle Rain • The Gift! (Recado Bossa Nova) • How Insensitive (Insensatez) • Once I Loved (Amor Em Paz) (Love in Peace) • Oye Como Va • Petite Fleur (Little Flower) • Slow Hot Wind (Lujon) • Só Danço Samba (Jazz 'N' Samba) • So Nice (Summer Samba) • Song for My Father • Sway (Quien Sera) • Sweet Happy Life (Samba de Orpheo) • Tico Tico (Tico Tico No Fuba) • Whatever Lola Wants.

00843242 B♭, E♭, C & Bass Clef Instruments $19.99

6. CHRISTMAS STANDARDS
Book/CD Pack

All I Want for Christmas Is My Two Front Teeth • Blue Christmas • Christmas Time Is Here • Do You Hear What I Hear • Feliz Navidad • Happy Holiday • Have Yourself a Merry Little Christmas • Here Comes Santa Claus (Right down Santa Claus Lane) • A Holly Jolly Christmas • I Saw Mommy Kissing Santa Claus • I'll Be Home for Christmas • Jingle-Bell Rock • Let It Snow! Let It Snow! Let It Snow! • Rudolph the Red-Nosed Reindeer • Santa Claus Is Comin' to Town • Silver and Gold • Silver Bells • Winter Wonderland.

00101397 B♭, E♭, C & Bass Clef Instruments $19.99

HAL•LEONARD® CORPORATION
7777 W. BLUEMOUND RD. P.O. BOX 13819 MILWAUKEE, WI 53213

Prices, content, and availability subject to change without notice.

0812